The Complete

Options

Trading Guide

The Complete Guide for Options Trading to Learn Strategies and Techniques, Making Money in Few Weeks.

Russell Bailey

TABLE OF CONTENTS

WHAT ARE THE BEST WAYS TO MAKE SUBSTANTIAL PROFITS THROUGH OPTION TRADING?

One successful fundamental thing and another successful thing will lead to a successful outcome. Let us venture into some of the ways that we need to get exposed to and consider so that our options trading activities can be successful.

Which Trading Is Profitable?

There are several basic kinds of options trading activities that the novice and even the experienced traders should be familiar with and get to master their favorite kinds of options trading that it is much going to be profitable during various occurrences. Here are some of the profitable ways.

1. Buy to open. This involves initiating a new order to secure a new option and eventually getting to improve on the existing trading position as judged from the past trading activities.
2. Sell to open. Selling to open is selling a specific option that you do not necessarily own and in the end, acquiring a new position or an improved position in the options trading activities.
3. Buying to close. This is buying a specific option that you

had previously sold in the market and eventually reducing a position in the options trading market.

4. Selling to close. In this kind of trading, an order to sell a specific option is exercised, where whatever you are selling had been previously been bought and end up reducing or exiting an existing position in the trading market.

How to Be A Successful Options Trader

Below are some of the ways we can shine on this options trading field.

1. Risk management. Life is a risk itself, implying that risks will always be depicted. An options trader needs to master all the possible ways in which he or she can minimize the number of risks that are likely to occur and learn from everyone of it for future good management. For instance, in the capital sector, the trader ought to have a big plan entailing details on how capital should be used strictly. Losses are also part of the options trading aftermath, and with bad capital handle, everything can tumble down. Think of how bad the market volatility can stand, leading to a great amount of capital, and leading to large chunks of losses.

2. Be the chief in numbers. Options trading involves wide use of numbers. Do you know the implied volatility? Is money in the option or out of the option? For beginners who have no single trace of what is going on, kindly commit oneself to some in-depth research and try to get a spotlight. For

the intermediate and experts, keep learning about various numbers in options trading. Life stops once you stop learning.

3. Possess great discipline. Self-discipline is encouraged as you get involved in options trading. This is the up-thrust motive force that will drive you towards as per your agenda plans with so much determination. You get to follow your specific laid plans and strategies, learn so much from your trading activities, and get the respective skills and experience for more successful options trading. Remember that your set plan strategies are the core objects during options trading, implying that self-discipline will bring you nothing but great success.

4. Great patience. Every aspect of life is a process led by constant growth. Trade during several market movements and get to learn from it. During this options trading journey, you will be exposed to various occurrences that you need to learn and master each one of them. Learn the possible risks involved, several market tricks and so much on. Well, get the best experience for it is always the best tutor.

5. Have your trading style. The intended trading style is what's normally implemented in the trading plan. Your trading style should be strictly adhered to and updated with new skills and information as you get involved in various options trading activities. Follow your plan without any other kind of influence and watch yourself grow with options trading.

6. A trading plans. Failing to plan is planning to fail. This implies that failing will only be reflected once planning does not happen. Successful options traders have big plans. Big plans entail good laid strategies, functions, discussions, in-depth research, great self-discipline, targets, and good goals. Establishing good trading plans is a clear reflection of great success in options trading.

7. Emotionally stable. Emotions can be quite a distraction as we get involved in different aspects of our lives. Losing a trade should be viewed just like a bad day that comes in handy with a good learning experience and knowledge for a bright future. Winning days should also be a learning day by valuing the good moves expressed that day.

8. Intensive learning and being proactive. Life always remains stagnant when you stop learning. Learning is achieved from the good side and the bad side, in that, master and learn every possible move expressed in options trading and be quite interested in picking the essence morals from the past episodes and squeezing any goodness from it. Also, subscribe to various well-contented channels and blogs to get the wide knowledge that is needed in options trading. Learning makes you informed and educated on the actual trade activities that are commonly involved in options trading.

9. Secure, accurate trading records. Try to learn from your mistakes though it can be tricky at times to formulate straight decisions based on your past performance since options trading is a matter of happy and sad seasons

governed by several set strategies that have been correctly laid in the options trading plan. It is encouraged to learn from your past mistakes and get to grow strategically to become a successful options trader.

10. Determination and commitment. This entails the high thrust force that should govern a beginner or any kind of experienced trader to acquire what is best for him or her in options trading and getting to know the several tips on becoming a successful options trader.

11. Be flexible. Another point to add is that when you feel that the market does not suit you at all that particular options trading period, find something constructive to do. Master any possible market move that is likely to take place in options trading and master it.

12. Basic understanding and interpretation. The trader should familiarize himself or herself with the basic market terminologies to understand the basic activities of the market and get to know the various ways on how to begin and handle option trading. Interpretation involves getting to analyze the actual options trading happenings in the market and sourcing the essentials in every trading activity. This helps the trader to always look out for the reality of the market rather than the hype and depending on the major market deadlines.

13. Be aggressive. Being aggressive in options trading necessarily implies that there is a thirst for great success, and the chances of acquiring large amounts of profits are so high. An aggressive option trader is mostly partaking

in-depth research learning new and learning new lucrative trading moves. This gives the trader much experience and skills to face any kind of risks that are likely to be involved in the market and, within no time, the trader has accredited a great expert in options trading.

14. Emotionally stable. The trader involved in options trading should not be controlled by various feelings experienced in the market. The losing days should not discourage the trader in any way such that he or she decides to stick with the market hype. It is highly recommended that traders should follow their plan and always stick to their various strategies.

15. Good stock pick. An options trader needs to pick the right option to sell. Weigh whether you are capable of handling the respective stock and managing the necessary risks highly involved in it. Most importantly, is the stock going to benefit the trader from acquiring large amounts of profits?

16. Good capital management. Money is significant when it comes to trading. Monitor and plan for every amount of capital you plan to utilize in the market. Always be careful in the amount of money you place in every option. Acquiring losses is always an alternative when it comes to option trading, a breakdown that can tumble you so badly and make you bankrupt as well. Plan for the capital you plan to invest in the company.

17. Powerful trading platforms. The kind of platform where various trading activities are taking place is pretty much

important in any kind of options trading involvement. Your best platform should consist of awesome navigation tools, learning sources, and other amazing features.

18. Selling options. Selling options is mostly preferred rather than buying options while practicing the call and put strategies that eventually help the trader to gain a good amount of profits.

19. Correct timing. As a trader, you should be informed of the good times and the bad times. Enter the market when the timing is quite favorable. Bad timing leads to great amounts of losses being made at the options trading market leading to a great downfall of finances. Bad timing leads to great amounts of losses being made at the options trading market leading to a great downfall of finances that, after all, cause bankruptcy.

OPTIONS VS STOCK TRADING VS. FOREX

There is a wide range of trading options available today in the market. In fact, most of us get confused while choosing the one on which we should invest our capital. We will be talking about some of the major differences between forex, stocks, and options.

Forex and Options

Forex Trading

Often known as FX trading or Foreign Currency Exchange, it is basically a market of finances where any person can easily trade the national currencies for making specific amounts of profits. Perhaps some people feel that the U.S. dollar will actually be stronger when compared to the British pound or euro. You can quickly develop a strategy for affecting this form of trade, and if your research turns out to be correct, you can actually make a good deal of profit.

In the case of options trading, you will be buying and selling options on large scale futures, stocks, etc. You can invest by determining whether the price will go up or down over a fixed time period. As with trading of Forex, one can easily leverage their power of buying for controlling a greater number of future or stock for instance, that he/she could generally have. But there are certain differences between options trading and forex which has been appropriately described below.

24 Hour Trading

An advantage that you can get with forex trading when compared to options trading is that you will be having the capability of trading for 24 hours in a day and five days in a week if you feel like. The market of forex is generally open for a more extended period of time than any other trading market. If your target is to make profits in double digits in the market, it is actually a great thing when you have an unlimited amount of time every week for making all those trades. Whenever any form of big event takes place anywhere in the world, you can turn out to be the first individual in taking full advantage of that very situation with the trading of forex. You are not required to wait for a long time for the market to open during the morning, as you would have to do in case of options trading. You have the power of trading directly from your PC, each and every hour of the day.

Rapid Execution of Trade

With the trading system of forex, you can receive immediate executions of trade. You will be facing no form of delay, which is in the case of options trading or for other forms of the market as well. Your order will get filled at the price that is best possible in place of just guessing the price in which you should fill up the order. The order of your choice will not just slip, which can happen with options trading. In forex trading, the rate of liquidity is a lot more for helping with the slippage which is present in trading of options.

No Commissions

X trading or forex trading is generally free from any form of commission. It is mainly because, in forex trading, everything takes place between banks that also match the buyers with the potential sellers and that too super quick. So, in short, in forex trading, the market is inter-bank. Thus, there are no signs of brokerage fees or middleman fees, which is the case with the other sort of markets. There is a huge spread between the asking price and the bid. This is where the firms of forex trading tend to make some of their profits. In options trading, you are required to pay out brokerage fees, whether you want to buy or sell. So, you can save a lot of money if you trade in forex markets when compared to the markets of options trading as there are no commissions.

Greater Leverage

In forex trading, you can get greater leverage when compared to options trading. But, with options trading, you will also be able to manage calls and put options in a way for greatly increasing the leverage. Leverage might turn out to be very important when you actually know what is going to be done by a currency. It is possible to achieve 200:1 or even greater in forex trading when compared to options trading, but it can also reach close. So, it can be said that with forex trading, one can make more profit if the right move is made.

Limited Nature of Risk Is Guaranteed

As the traders of forex need to have limits of position, the risk associated with it is also limited as the capabilities of the online system of forex trading can automatically start a margin call when the amount of margin turns out to be much greater than the account value in dollars. This helps the traders of forex from losing not so much if, by chance, their very own position tends to go the other way. It is actually a great feature of safety, which is not available all the time in other markets of financing. How are options different from forex in this aspect? In the options aspect, you can only have a limited amount of time for trading right before the expiration of the options.

Higher Variability

In forex trading markets, the rate of variability is much higher, and thus, it can result in more risk for the traders. In the markets of forex, the traders are required to decide the direction in which their assets will be going and also have to predict low or high the assets will go. So, it can be stated that the ultimate profit and risk are completely unknown. In forex trading, there are no barriers to the amount of money that the traders can lose or make, until and unless they start using certain tools for controlling their trading. One of such tools is a stop loss, which helps in preventing the traders from not losing more than a specific amount of money. In simple terms, once the related trader has already lost a certain amount of money, the trade will be closed automatically. The maximum loss that someone can have in forex trading is all the money that they have in their account of trading.

This is not the case with options trading. It is all about the strike price and expiry time where the traders lose only a certain amount of money, nothing big.

While considering the primary differences between options trading and forex trading, always remember your very own style of trading and the risk type that you will be able to handle. There are obvious advantages in forex trading as well as in options trading that can permit you to gain a good amount of profit. But this can only be achieved if you can develop a system that is functional and that can stay within the limits of your trading. So, for becoming a successful trader, you first need to properly learn the major differences between the two markets of trading.

Stocks and Options

If you want to be a successful investor, you will need to have a proper understanding of the various opportunities for investment first. Most people allow their advisors of investment to take the decisions instead of them. While talking about opportunities of investing, options and stocks are two of the most common markets of investment. Both are indeed traded similarly, but they still lie some differences between the two. Stock is an instrument of financing. It shows up ownership of a business, and it also helps in signifying a proper claim on the business profits and assets. In simple terms, when you have the stocks of a certain company, you own a part of it, which is proportional to the total share numbers that the company has. For instance, when you own about 100 shares of a company that has in total 1000 shares, you own 10% of that company.

Well, as you already know, options are the contracts of selling or buying an asset at a fixed price and within a fixed time. Unlike the case of stocks, the contracts of options will not provide you with direct ownership of any company, but it will permit you with the right of selling and buying a great number of the stocks of the company.

Leveraged Profits

The holders of options contracts can take full advantage of the leveraged nature of profits. For instance, when the price of any stock rises by one percent, the price of the options is most likely to rise by ten percent. So, it can be stated that the profits of options are ten times more than the stock price in this case.

Limitation of Time

Options come with a limited time frame. Thus, options can be held by any holder of option only till the expiration time. But, in the case of stocks, if the user opts for a short or long position, he/she can keep the stock for an indefinite frame of time.

Movement of Price

When there is variation in the overall price of any stock, the price of the options will also tend to vary. But, the value variation of the options is comparatively low. The extent of how close the variation of price of the options matches along with the variation of stock variation can be calculated by the strike price which is generally defined in the contract of options.

Worthless Expiry

The primary reason why a majority of the people who are holders of options end up in losing their entire investments in a short period of time is mainly that all these derivatives tend to end up with a worthless nature of expiry in case the underlying assets fail to perform in the way as expected within a fixed time frame. That is the reason why the trading of all these instruments of finance is considered as a high profit-high risk activity. But, if you end up buying stocks, you have the power of keeping all the underlying securities within your portfolio as long as you want them to if the price of the same does not tend to rise. It is possible to easily benefit from the rise in the price of stocks even if it takes several years to happen.

Price

In this world, everyone is trying to save money. In that case, options are much cheaper when compared to stocks. But, in the case of stocks, they are very expensive. Each contract of an option can gives you overall control of about 100 shares of equity, but still, the cost that is needed for purchasing contracts of options is actually far away from the expense of buying an equal amount of stock.

LEARN THE TERMINOLOGY OF TRADING

The Options Jargons

So, turning out to be familiar requires learning some key terms. Here are the basics for starting financial specialists to exchange options.

Strike Price

For one to know whether a stock can be worked out, the strike cost would need to be gauged. There is a value that it should have when a choice gets to the expiry date. This cost ought to be lower or higher than the stock cost, and the strike cost of a basic resource is the thing that we allude to like that. In the event that you expect, as a financial specialist, that the estimation of the stock will rise, you can purchase a call alternative at a value set for the strike. With regards to putting options, the expense of a call will be the cost at which the alternative holder will exchange an advantage when the agreement terminates. The strike cost, as well, perhaps called the activity cost. It is a really critical factor to consider when choosing the estimation of the alternative. The strike cost can change, as indicated by when the options are executed. As a financial specialist, monitoring the strike cost is something to be thankful for as it assists with distinguishing the proficiency of speculation.

Styles

There are two basic models of styles. Those are styles of European and American options. On the off chances or opportunities that you wish to exchange options, it is fitting to outfit yourself with information on the various sorts. You will perceive those that work for you when you assess the models and those that don't. Once in a while, you'll see that particular models are less difficult to comprehend and oversee than others. You may select to take part in the one that is simple for you and quit taking part in a difficult situation understanding.

The American-style choice permits one to exchange any period between the hour of procurement and the hour of expiry of an agreement. Due to its benefit, most dealers take part in this style. This expects one to play out the exchange at any period during which an agreement is viewed as authentic. Contrasted and the American style, the European style choice isn't broadly utilized. A broker can just exercise his/her options during the lapse date in the European choice organization. On the off chances that you aren't an option exchanging master, I would encourage you not to utilize the European kind.

Date of Termination

A termination date alludes to the time after which an agreement is viewed as void. The period between the time they were bought and the expiry date shows a choice's legitimacy. As a seller, during this time range, you should utilize the agreements for your potential benefit. You can trade as much as possible, and get exceptional yields over the purchasing time frame and expiry period. Figure out how to utilize the time accessibly. On the off chances that you are not cautious, the privilege can lapse before you are allowed an opportunity to practice it.

We will have starters who have faith in this angle and wind up losing gradually. Taking part in the financial exchange would permit you to be mindful. Neglecting to take a gander at the expiry date will prompt your stocks to be esteemed useless without getting an opportunity to put resources into them. The inventories are practiced before the expiry time frame in certain strange cases.

Contracts

Agreements apply to the number of offers that individual intends to buy. One hundred offers in a basic resource compare to an agreement. Agreements help in choosing the estimation of the stock. Agreements will, in general, be significant until the date of expiry. An agreement might be considered invalid after the expiry date. Realizing this will assist you in finding the correct opportunity to pound out an arrangement. For a situation where a broker is purchasing ten options, the individual in question gets 10 $350 calls. If stock qualities go over $350, the seller gets a chance to buy or sell 1000 portions of their stock at $350, at the expiry rate. This happens to pay little mind to the stock cost at that specific time. On an occasion that the stock is underneath $350, the choice terminates uselessly. As a speculator, that will bring about an all-out misfortune. You'll lose the entire sum you used to purchase options, and it is extremely unlikely you can get it back. In case you're trying to put resources into exchanging options, it's fundamental to get mindful of the agreements and how you can practice them for a fruitful exchanging result.

Premium

The premium is right to the cash you used to buy options. You will get the reward by increasing the cost of a call and the number of agreements by 100. The '100' mirrors the number of offers per bargain.

At the point when you choose to take part in stocks, you will run over different terms. We have numerous individuals putting intensely in stocks since they couldn't comprehend the various terms utilized. Not that ought to be the situation. You should set aside some effort to experience the words and completely consider what they mean.

The Right, However, Not the Commitment

What strikes a chord when perusing this announcement? All things considered, when we talk or have rights, we mean you have the opportunity to purchase such an item. At this point, when we talk about obligation, we apply to the way that one has no legitimate position to play out an obligation. Options don't allow dealers a legitimate option to lead an assignment. This implies the opportunity of exchange exists, yet it isn't lawfully authorized.

Selling or Buying

You are given the options to purchase or trade an alternative as a dealer. There are two kinds of stock from which one can pick. We have the chance to position and the alternative to call. Both recognize, and each has its upsides and downsides.

Setting Explicit Price

There is a particular value set for practicing the right. The cost will shift, as indicated by the kind of item. Some investment opportunities will, in general, be more costly than others. There is an assortment of elements influencing the options rates. At the point when you keep on perusing this book, these angles will come through to you. Realizing them can permit you to comprehend when to lead an exchange, and when not to make an exchange, contingent upon the effect of the components; an exchange can create a high salary or result in misfortune.

Expiry of The Agreement

The expiry date is the point at which an agreement is viewed as useless. Investment opportunities are dated to expiry. The year is set to choose the estimation of choice. Correspondence will be esteemed to be current whenever before the expiry date. This guarantees it tends to be utilized at any phase before the expiry date to deliver incomes. At the point when the expiry date is reached, a merchant has no capacity to practice the right. That is on the grounds that the agreement is viewed as useless. As a financial specialist, it's indispensable to guarantee your venture is reliably inside its legitimacy range.

HOW TO PROPERLY MANAGE A TRADE

Managing Risk in Options Trading

Appropriate hazard control in alternatives trading may additionally sound like an outdated idea to some people; however, the truth is that effective threat management is the primary recipe for fulfillment in alternatives trading. Being capable of manipulating your risk exposure in addition to your capital effectively is fundamental when trading alternatives. In as plenty as the hazard is essentially unavoidable in any enterprise venture, the exposure to hazard must not be a problem. The key solution is to take measures to manipulate the budget, which are at threat efficaciously. Always ensure which you consent to the degree of hazard you're exposing your trade to and that you do not reveal yourself to untenable losses.

Use Your Trading Master Plan

It is critical to be in ownership of a complete trading grasp plan that designs the parameters as well as recommendations for the exchange. The most practical makes use of this type of plan include money management and, most importantly, in this case, coping with your publicity to chance. Your trading the plan ought to be which contain detailed information on the diploma of hazard that you are comfortable with in addition to the quantity of capital you plan to make investments with.

When you follow your plan to the letter and strictly use the funds that have been categorically set apart for the motive of options trading, it becomes smooth to fend off a number of the greatest mistakes that traders and traders make, such as, investing the usage of finances that are "scared".

The second you prefer to change the use of price range which you ought to have allocated to other uses or price range that you can't come up with the money for to divest, probabilities are that you will not make logical decisions for your trading activities. Whereas it is hard to put off emotions that come forth in options trading entirely, you desperately need to consciousness as a whole lot as viable in your trading sports. Why?

As soon as feelings crush you, possibilities are that you may start dropping your consciousness and consequently behave irrationally. For instance, you could be driven to perform transactions that you could, in any other case, no longer have made in ordinary circumstances. However, in fact, you strictly work according to the design of your trading plan and strictly use the assets you allocated to investment, then the possibilities are that you'll take control of your feelings.

You need to abide by using the diploma of hazard additionally strictly. This is said inside the trading plan. Giving your consent to trades, which might be low threat means that you ought to chorus from setting yourself in positions to disclose you to more significant dangers. Usually, it's miles tempting to put yourself in inclined positions using exposing yourself to risk in case you make a couple of losses and yet you're inside the quest to make things proper, or perhaps you've got performed noticeably properly with several low-risk trades, and you have the preference to revamp your profits at a far faster. If your choice becomes to settle for minimal chance investment, there is truly no want to go out of your safe zone using falling prey to the emotions.

Using Option Spreads to Manage Risks

Option spreads may be termed as useful and essential instruments each time you're trading in alternatives. Options spreads are necessary each time you integrate multiple roles on options agreements about similar protection required to come up with a standard role of trade effectively.

An instance might be making a buy in the money calls on a positive inventory then going in advance to write out of money calls, which might be cheaper on that inventory. Doing because of this, you will have given you a form of spread that is usually referred to as the bull spread. Purchasing calls insinuates that you are in a position to make gains if the value of the basic stock upsurges. However, you will lose a section of or all the finances used to buy them if it occurs that the inventory's fee failed to rise. When you favor writing, calls based on that equal stock, you'll have the capability to take management of some of the costs you incurred, to begin with, and therefore cut down the total amount of budget you may have lost.

Virtually all the techniques of alternatives trading call for spreads to be used and those spreads are a representation of an efficient way to mitigate the danger. They can also be used to cut down the upfront prices of moving into a position and lessening the range of finances you're in a function to lose, similar to inside the bull spread. This essentially means which you possibly cut down the earnings you should have made but ultimately coping with the trendy risk.

Spreads are equally vital when anyone seeks to reduce the risks that come each time you input a role. This is short. It is viable to get into positions that present you with a threat to advantage income if the charges move for you want, however, you could effectively limit any losses you will have incurred if the motion of charges did now not desire you. This explains why very many options buyers use spreads; they're magnificent equipment for threat control.

There is a wide variety of spreads that can take management of really any situation that the marketplace brings forth.

Risk Management Through Diversification

Being varied is a tool used to control dangers via investors who're creating a group of shares through a method of purchasing and holding. The underlying criterion of being assorted for this form of traders is the dissemination of trades to a variety of various sectors and agencies and building up a portfolio that is balanced instead of having a whole lot of price range stacked up together in a single sector or company. A portfolio this is varied is broadly taken into consideration to have minimal publicity to threat in assessment to a portfolio. This is composed of particularly one particular sort of investment.

Nonetheless, it still has a variety of uses that you may use to perform diversification in several different approaches. In as a great deal because the precept mostly stays unchanged, you must now not have a variety of capital tied to one particular type of investment.

Diversification can be carried out the usage of selected and varying techniques by way of executing trading alternatives, which might be established on a sequence of essential securities, as well as ensuring that you exchange in a selection of options. The goal at the back of being varied is that you can make income in distinctive ways and that you do not entirely rely on one particular final result for the fulfillment of all of your trading ventures.

Risk Management Using Option Orders

A comparatively smooth manner to mitigate chance is to utilize the numerous orders that you have the capacity to location. To upload to the four key order types which might be used in close and open positions, there is a chain of more orders that can be placed, and the bulk of these may be instrumental in handling risks.

For instance, a regular order inside the marketplace will be complete upon the provision of the finest rate during threat implementation. It is an excellently basic technique of promoting in addition to buying options, however, in turbulent markets, possibilities are that your order may get complete at either lower or higher rate than how you expected it turn out.

Also, some orders can be used in making the method of exiting a role automatically. This is regardless of whether its pursuits at locking in profit that has been made or cutting losses on trading activities whose consequences were now not favorable. Making use of orders like the trailing stop order or marketplace stop order, you bought the ability to determine the factor to go away a role easily.

This system will be crucial in helping you avoid situations wherein you do no longer get income because you stuck in a single function for an exceptionally long period or go through losses due to the fact you did not close out on an unfavorable role fast enough. When you use option orders in the right manner, you may minimize the threat you get uncovered to any time you alternate.

The Bottom Line

Very many folks who are new to the sphere of options trading make a gruesome mistake of blindly investing quite a few their money in their enterprise ventures. This exposes them to a chain of dangers, which include the loss of good-sized quantities of difficult-earned money. Therefore, figuring out the proper amount of budget to use as capita and the way to use it in options trading gives the investor the potential to free up the capacity of leverage. The fundamental solution to dealing with being uncovered to risk is to ask yourself several "what if" questions, and as you do so, make sure which you use danger tolerance because of the guiding factor.

THE ADVICE OF THE BEST INVESTORS IN THE WORLD

There is more to options day trading to just having a style or a strategy. If that was all it took, then you could adopt those that are proven to work and stick with them. Yes, options day trading styles and strategy are essential, but they are not the end-all-be-all of this career.

The winning factor is the options day trader himself or herself. You are the factor that determines whether or not you will win or lose in this career. Only taking the time to develop your expertise, seeking guidance when necessary, and being dedicated allows a person to move from a novice options day trader to an experienced one that is successful and hitting his or her target goals.

To develop into the options day trader you want to be, being disciplined is necessary. There are options day trading rules that can help you develop that essential discipline. You will make mistakes. Every beginner in any niche does and even experienced options day traders are human and thus, have bad days too.

Knowing common mistakes helps you avoid many of these mistakes and takes away much of the guesswork. Having rules to abide by enables you to avoid these mistakes as well.

Below, I have listed six rules that every option day trader must know. Following them is entirely up to you, but know that they are proven to help beginner options day trader turn into winning options day traders.

Have Realistic Expectations

It is sad to say that many people who enter the options trading industry are doing so to make a quick buck. Options trading is not a get-rich-quick scheme. It is a reputable career that has made many people rich, but that is only because these people have put in the time, effort, study, and dedication to learning the craft and mastering it. Mastery does not happen overnight, and beginner options day traders need to be prepared for that learning curve and to have the courage to stick with day trading options even when it becomes severe.

Losses are also part of the game. No trading style or strategy will guarantee gains all the time. The best options traders have a winning percentage of about 80% and a losing average of approximately 20%. That is why an options day trader needs to be a good money manager and a good risk manager. Be prepared for eventual losses and be ready to minimize those losses.

Start Small to Grow a Big Portfolio

Caution is the name of the game when you just get started with day trading options. Remember that you are still learning options trading and developing an understanding of the financial market. Do not jump the gun even if you are eager. After you have practiced paper trading, start with smaller options positions, and steadily grow your standing as you get a lay of the options day trading land. This strategy allows you to keep your losses to a minimum and to develop a systematic way of entering positions.

Know Your Limits

You may be tempted to trade as much as possible to develop a winning monthly average, but that strategy will have the opposite effect and land you with a losing average. Remember that every options trader needs careful consideration before that contract is set up. Never overtrade and tie up your investment fund.

Be Mentally, Physically and Emotionally Prepared Every Day

This is a mentally, physically, and emotionally tasking career, and you need to be able to meet the demands of this career. That means keeping your body, mind, and heart in good health at all times. Ensure that you schedule time for self-care every day. That can be as simple as taking the time to read for recreation to having elaborate self-care routine carved out in the evenings.

Not keeping your mind, heart, and head in optimum health means that they are more likely to fail you. Signs that you need to buckle up and care for yourself more diligently include being constantly tired, being short-tempered, feeling preoccupied, and being easily distracted.

To ensure you perform your best every day, here a few tasks that you need to perform:

- Get the recommended amount of sleep daily. This is between 7 and 9 hours for an adult.
- Practice a balanced diet. The brain and body need adequate nutrition to work their best. Include fruits, complex carbs, and veggies in this diet and reduce the consumption of processed foods.
- Eat breakfast lunch and dinner every day. Fuel your mind and body with the main meals. Eating a healthy breakfast is especially important because it helps set the tone for the rest of the day.
- Exercise regularly. Being inactive increases your risk of developing chronic diseases like heart disease, certain cancers, and other terrible health consequences. Adding just a few minutes of exercise to your daily routine not only reduces those risks but also allows your brain to function better, which is a huge advantage for an options day trader.
- Drink alcohol in moderation or not at all.
- Stop smoking.
- Reduce stress contributors in your environment.

Analyze Your Daily Performance

To determine if the options day trading style and strategies that you have adopted are working for you, you need to track your performance. At the most basic, this needs to be done on a daily basis by virtue of the fact that you are trading options daily. This will allow you to notice patterns in your profit and loss. This can lead to you determining the why and how of these gains and losses. These determinations lead to fine tuning your daily processes for maximum returns.

Pay Attention to Volatility

Volatility speaks to how likely a price change will occur over a specific amount of time on the financial market. Volatility can work for an options day trader or against the options day trader. It all depends on what the options day trader is trying to accomplish and what his or her current position is.

There are many external factors that affect volatility, and such factors include the economic climate, global events, and news reports. Strangles and straddles strategies are great for use in volatile markets.

There are different types of volatility, and they include:

- Price volatility, which describes how the price of an asset increases or decreases based on the supply and demand of that asset.
- Historical volatility, which is a measure of how an asset has performed over the last 12 months.
- Implied volatility, which is a measure of how an asset will perform in the future.

Be Flexible

Many options day traders find it difficult to try trading styles and strategies that they are not familiar with. While the saying of, "Do not fix it if it is not broken," is quite true, you will never become more effective and efficient in this career if you do not step out of your comfort zone at least once in a while. Yes, stick with want work but allow room for the consideration that there may be better alternatives.

WHAT IS THE RIGHT MENTAL ATTITUDE?

The options trader mentality

To avoid making these types of errors, it's miles essential to undertake trading psychology. In short, this means having a strict plan which you follow at all times. In a sense, you need to be detached from your trading on an emotional level, as in case you were not the one risking the cash. Of course, this isn't always usually clean to do. If you are losing your difficult-earned money, it can be difficult to detach yourself emotionally from what's going on.

The manner of doing that is to set up rules beforehand of time and comply with them. As a part of your trading psychology, becoming organized and disciplined goes to be something that you need to master. If you are not the individual who is organized and prone to detailed making plans, then you definitely will need to alter your method to things.

A critical part of trading psychology isn't always giving into emotion. As we referred to within the introduction, you could fly right into a panic when you get significant losses, and you could also become excessively happy while you get gains. When you allow emotion to guide your trading selections, you're going to locate which you make several errors. Sometimes, luck might be worried, and so investors who are vulnerable to making emotional selections and not cautiously planning out their trades are nevertheless going to have a few spectacular wins. This helps to maintain them addicted and convey them returned to make many trades. If they get a significant winning exchange, it'll inspire them to keep following the same impulsive procedure hoping to hit another big win.

First-rate trading psychology is one that starts with an extended-term plan. You need to take a seat down and figure out what your lengthy-time period dreams are over exceptional time frames. First off, you want to be questioning in terms of reasonable gains. You are not likely to build fulfillment by way of hoping to make a million dollars right away. Instead, think in terms of making $one hundred a week or $200 a week. Then map out a method this is going that will help you virtually realize your dreams. Then once you have reached the goal, you can set a new purpose to boom your income.

Trading alternatives is not something that you may do if you have a "set it and forget about it" attitude. As an alternative's trader, even though you don't necessarily have to be glued to your computer all day long, you want to be carefully monitoring the actions in the proportion charge of any underlying inventory for your alternatives. You don't need to impulsively purchase an option (or ten options) and then burst off and overlook approximately them. You have to be regularly checking to peer how your alternatives are doing and likely the use of electronic tools to set up indicators and so forth.

Trading Journal

It is my perception that each option trader has to maintain a written file of their sports in a trading journal. Start the journal by using mapping out your goals for the next three months. Include the quantity of cash you want to earn and broaden a plan to reach your intention. Then consist of a report of all your trades within the journal. Include the date you input the change, how many options you got or sold, and the amount of capital involved. Then while you close out your exchange, replace your entries with the very last effects. It is essential to hold a record and be honest with yourself. One of the errors that impulsive and emotional traders make is that they don't keep a report of their real trades. That makes it smooth to idiot yourself into wondering that you are breaking even or even making some earnings, while, in fact, you are dropping cash.

You need to additionally hold a record of your effects, including income and losses for each exchange and some other expenses. This may be stored in written shape or with the aid of the usage of a spreadsheet. This will help you decide whether or not or no longer you have got a triumphing trading program and recognize your real net advantage or loss. It is essential to be realistic approximately where you are and how properly you are doing in reaching your desires and keeping a detailed file as opposed to winging its miles one manner of doing that.

If you locate which you continuously have losing trades, then you definitely shouldn't keep doing what you've been doing. Obviously, in the beginning, you could anticipate losing money on numerous of your first trades probably, and you might lose money on multiple trades in a row. That is pleasant inside the first few weeks of trading, but if you find after a month, you're continually losing money on your trades, you will want to take a step lower back and do some evaluation to find out the reasons why you maintain dropping on trades. Write down everything approximately the exchange, along with how long you stayed inside the trade, what made you pick the change, how lots become invested, and so on. Are you keeping on too long? Getting out too prematurely? Investing in alternatives proper before earnings calls and getting hammered with the aid of bad decisions? Getting in on a rising stock rate too late, handiest to find that you mistimed it, and the stock fee began dropping soon when you entered into your positions?

When you do your evaluation and provide you with some changes to your trading technique, then you may resume trading with an up to date training plan. Keep in mind that that is a work in progress, and you don't must expect success immediately.

Be Realistic: It Isn't All Wins

Many buyers think they're not doing properly if they don't win on every change. The truth is that even the nice alternatives traders are going to experience losses. The aim is to win greater often than you lose so that you have net profits. Over time as you advantage revel in, you can count on to improve your performance.

Value Education

Those who are inclined to look at and learn are, without a doubt, going to be a higher success than those who honestly start trading on impulse. There are many assets to be had for the ones who want to change alternatives, and also, you need to take gain of them usually. The more that you could examine alternatives trading, the more possibly it's far that you're going to be a success. You ought to watch as many videos as you can find, examine all of the specific methods and techniques that may be used while trading alternatives, and study as many educational substances as possible.

It would help if you searched for official statistics approximately options that let you learn the ropes from experienced buyers. Many companies that can be associated with options trading have educational substances to be had. I also strongly recommend that you observe a tasty change. This is a group associated with the alternatives trading platform Tasty Works, but you don't must have an account with Tasty Works to use the academic platform. They have a significant quantity of educational videos that might be free to view on their internet site and YouTube. They also talk indicates wherein they speak different trading effects, approaches to trading, and interviews with individuals who became successful options buyers. Since it's free and put together by using people who have been professional alternatives buyers for many years in some cases, this is one of the first-class assets that you could use to teach yourself approximately trading options.

WHAT ARE THE BIGGEST FEARS PEOPLE HAVE WHEN THEY START TRADING OPTIONS?

Fear

At any given time, fear represents one of the worst kinds of emotions that you can have. Check-in your newspaper one day, and you read about a steep selloff, and the next thing is trying to rack your brain about what to do next, even if it isn't the right action at that time.

Many investors think that they know what will happen in the next few days, which makes them have a lot of confidence in the outcome of the trade. This leads to investors getting into the trade at a level that is too high or too low, which in turn makes them react emotionally.

As the trader puts a lot of hope on the single trade, the level of fear tends to increase, and hesitation and caution kick in.

Fear is part of every trader, but skilled traders can manage fear. There are various types of fears that you will experience, let us look at a few of them:

The Fear to Lose

Have you ever entered a trade and all you could think about is losing? The fear of losing makes it hard for you to execute the perfect strategy or enter or exit a strategy at the right time.

As a trader, you know that you need to make timely decisions when the strategy signals you to take one. When fear is guiding you, the level of confidence drops, and you can't execute the strategy the right way, at the right time. When a strategy fails, you lose trust in your abilities as well as strategy.

When you lose trust in many of the strategies, you end up with analysis paralysis, whereby you can't pull the trigger on any decision that you make. Making a move becomes a huge challenge.

When you cannot pull the trigger, all you can think about is staying away from the pain of losing, while you need to move towards gains.

No trader likes to lose, but it is a fact that even the best traders will make losses once in a while. The key is for them to make more profitable trades that allow them to stay in the game.

When you worry too much, you end up being distracted from your execution process, and instead, you focus on the results.

To reduce the fear of trading, you need to accept losses. The probability of losing or making a profit is 50/50, and you need to accept this fact and accept a trade, whether it is a sell or a buy signal.

The Fear of a Positive Trend Going Negative (and Vice Versa)

Many traders choose to go for quick profits and then leave the losses to run down. Many traders want to convince themselves that they have made some money for the day, so they tend to go for a quick profit so that they have the winning feeling.

So, what should you do instead? It would help if you stuck with the trend. When you notice a trend is starting, it is good to stay with the trend until you have a signal that the trend is about to reverse. It is only then that you exit this position.

To understand this concept, you need to consider the history of the market. History is good at pointing out that times change, and trends can go either way. Remember that no one knows the exact time the trend will start or end; all you need to do is wait upon the signal.

The Fear of Missing Out

For every trade, you have people that doubt the capacity of the trade to go through. After you place the trade, you will be faced with many skeptics that will doubt the whole procedure and leave you wondering whether to exit the strategy or not.

This fear is also characterized by greed – because you aren't working on the premise of making a successful trade rather the fact that the security is rising without you having a piece of the pie.

This fear is usually based on information that there is a trend that you missed that you would have capitalized on.

This fear has a downside – you will forget about any potential risk associated with the trade and instead think that you can make a profit because other people benefited from the action.

Fear of Being Wrong

Many traders put too much emphasis on being right that they forget that this is a business they should run the right way. They also forget that being successful is all about knowing the trend and how it affects their engagement.

When you follow the best timing strategy, you create many positive results over a certain time.

The uncanny desire to focus on always being right instead of focusing on making money is a great part of your ego, and to stay on the right path; you need to trade without your ego for once.

If you accommodate a perfectionist mentality when you get into trades, you will be after failure because you will experience a lot of losses as well. Perfectionists don't take losses the right way, and this translates into fear.

Ways to Overcome Fear in Trading

As you can see, it is obvious that fear can lead to losses. So, how can you avoid this fear and become successful?

- **Learn**

You need to find a way to get knowledge so that you have the basis for making decisions. When you know all there is to know about options, you know what to buy and when to sell, and learn which ones to watch. You are then more comfortable making the right decisions.

- **Have Goals**

What are your short term and long-term goals? Setting the right goals helps you to overcome fear. When you have goals, you have rules that dictate how you behave, even in times of fear. You also have a timeline for your journey.

- **Envision the Bigger Picture**

You always need to evaluate your choices at all times and see what you have gained or lost so far for taking some steps. Understanding the mistakes, you made gives you guidance to make better decisions in the future.

- **Start Small**

Many traders that subscribe to fear have lost a lot before.

They put a lot of funds on the line and ended up losing, which in turn made them fear to place other trades. Begin with small sums so that you don't risk too much to put fear in you. Once you get more confident, you can invest larger sums so that you enjoy more profit.

- **Use the Right Strategy**

Having the right trading strategy makes it easy to execute your trades successfully. Make sure you look at various options trading strategies so that you know which one is ideal for your situation and skills.

Many strategies can help you succeed, but others might leave you confused. If you have a strategy that doesn't give you the returns you desire, then adjust it to suit your needs over time. Refine it till you are comfortable with its performance.

- **Go Simple**

When you have a strategy that is simple and straightforward, you will be less likely to lose confidence along the way because you know what to expect.

Additionally, the easier the strategy, the faster it will be to spot any issues.

- **Don't Hesitate**

At times you have to jump into the fray even if you aren't so comfortable with the way it works. Once you begin taking steps, you will learn more about the trade.

However, you need always to be prepared when taking

any trade. The more prepared you are, the easier it will be for you to run successful trades.

- **Don't Give Up**

Things might not always go as you expect them to do. Remember that mistakes are there to give you lessons that will make you a better trader. When you lose, take time to identify the mistake you made and then correct it, then try again.

Greed

This refers to a selfish desire to get more money than you need from a trade. When the desire to get more than you can usually make takes over your decision-making process, you are looking at failure.

Greed is seen to be more detrimental than fear. Yes, fear can make you lose trades, but the good thing is that you get to preserve your capital. On the other hand, greed places you in a situation where you spend your capital faster than you return it. It pushes you to act when you shouldn't be acting at all.

The Danger of Being Greedy

When you are greedy, you end up acting irrationally. Irrational trading behavior can be overtrading, overleveraging, holding onto trades for too long, or chasing different markets.

The more greed you have, the more foolish you act. If you reach a point at which greed takes over from common sense, then you are overdoing it.

When you are greedy, you also end up risking way much more than you can handle, and you end up with a loss. You also have unrealistic expectations from the market, which makes it seem as if you are after just money and nothing else.

When you are greedy, you also start trading prematurely without any knowledge of the options trading market.

When you are too greedy, your judgment is clouded, and you won't think about any negative consequences that might result when you make certain decisions.

Many traders that were too greedy ended up giving up after making this mistake in the initial trading phase.

How to Overcome Greed

Like any other endeavor in trading, you need a lot of effort to overcome greed. It might not be easy because we are talking about human emotions here, but it is possible.

First, you have to know that every call you make won't be the right one at all times. There are times when you won't make the right move, and you will end up losing money. At times you will miss the perfect strategy altogether, and you won't move a step ahead.

Secondly, you have to agree that the market is way bigger than you. When you do this, you will accept and make mistakes in the process.

Hope

Hope is what keeps a trading expectation alive when it has reached reversal. Hope is usually factored in the mind of a trader that has placed a huge amount on a trade. Many traders also go for hope when they wish to recoup past losses. These traders are always hopeful that the next trade will be the best, and they end up placing more than they should on the trade.

This type of emotion is dangerous because the market doesn't care at all about your hopes and will take your money.

Regret

This is the feeling of disappointment or sadness over a trade that has been done, especially when it has resulted in a loss.

Focusing too much on missing on trade makes the trader not to move forward. After you learn the lessons after such a loss, you need to understand the mistakes you made then move ahead.

How Option Prices Are Determined

Optional trading has grown extensively, even within the selling of shares. The buyers in this marketplace care approximately the future growth of the commercial enterprise and no longer the existing as opposed to the same old stock exchange. In this exercise, one acquires the right to buy a stock however, not the obligation. However, it ought to be earlier than a positive maturation length. By the word obligation, its method that you aren't mandated or forced to buy, however, is elective. This practice is an agreement as it has the maturation length which the trader ought to comply with.

You ought to recognize the critical definition of a number of the phrases of this trading. These terms will prove considerable in understanding the charge trend of this trade. Remember that your important aim within the business is to have much less price destiny contracts of buying an asset. You need to observe keenly on records regarding the property to transact because their amount depends on lots on the premium you pay. The following are some of the terms determined in this marketplace.

There is a capped fashion alternative. This enterprise is generally practiced while you are already privy to the asset's charge. Therefore, you could quickly examine the profit you'll advantage of the give up of the maturation date. The chance of trading is also significantly reduced, and you could take a look at the right amount to apply for the commercial enterprise.

Always bear in mind that this enterprise is associated with forecasting of the destiny price and having the proper to buy the belongings with no obligation. However, you may marvel who facilitates such actions. It is not a broker as many of you might imagine, however, is an alternative creator. In simple, this man or woman might also be called the vendor of an option. He or she is the mastermind of the whole procedure and will direct you on the way to calculate the maturity fee.

The character also is in the rate of receiving the top rate. One extra component with him is that he is obliged to buy the property or the underlying safety on the mandated fee.

Sometimes because of the volatility of the marketplace, you fear that the market will elapse considerably. There you make the right call via deciding on the alternatives trading. If you're that guy, who postpones the trading with the wish that it will preserve its worth at the expense of a volatile market, then you're mistaken. Therefore, recognize which you are practicing the name options. This method is crucial if you assume that the marketplace for the shares is going to upward thrust past your budget.

Another factor is the positioned alternative that's vice versa of the call option. That involves the vendor of the shares who fears that the stock marketplace will recede. Therefore, that vendor will exercise the mandate to promote stocks at a special rate at a destiny date. In this case, the stock fee falls below the next quantity.

That future price is known as the strike fee. It is for that reason the fee this is realized at that scheduled times, which the client or seller expects. More honest to say, is the price bought or bought over that specified length wherein you made both a name or put option. That price typically is exercised earlier than the contract matures.

Everyone deserves the credit score for their paintings, even the option author too. Therefore, that credit score is steeply-priced in terms of payments. You have to pay that individual an elective premium. That price is realized consistent with the settlement between you and the non-compulsory author. That proper you are shopping for or promoting, you have to stable it with the charges paid. Otherwise, it will likely be reserved for anyone else.

You have to gauge the profit you will take within the non-obligatory trading. Therefore, some terms, like the intrinsic price, should no longer break out your ears. This fee is calculated by using subtracting the price of the underlying stocks with the strike charge. Remember that this trading is a spinoff organ that depends on the quantity of the fundamental asset. That fundamental has its market index, which ought to be less in case of call up or much less in the case has put up an alternative.

The extrinsic fee is another extensive segment in this kind of marketplace. It is the cost of that right against the intrinsic price. This trading usually seems like a time fee fixture that has fewer profits.

Assumptions and Consideration of Optional Pricing

One assumption is that the underlying charge of the stock is calmly distributed. That way, the logarithm in operating on its value is constant. By doing so, you could anticipate what's going to be the strike price or the predicted cost of the belongings. In other terms, the volatility and the trend of the market are specific. Recognize that the volatility is the pointy increase and decrease within the rate of an inventory. The scheme additionally makes the mathematical calculation of the top class and the intrinsic price operational due to that constant function.

There aren't any transaction fees found out on this avenue. Moreover, there are not any taxes evaluated, which can be calculated alongside the striking cost. Otherwise, the tax and transaction charges will affect the intrinsic cost reached. Therefore, by way of including those inside the final price, there can be a sensitivity to the change in the economic instruments. Value relative to the charge of the underlying belongings.

There are not any dividends too on this safety. The bonus would operate similar to the taxes and transaction expenses. That is to mean, if they may be included, the final value can be one-of-a-kind from the anticipated. They, too, need to be paid per year, and it's far sensible to cast off the dividends so that one can attain the accurate outcomes.

The risks of free charge are believed as regular. This price is generally associated with government subsidies or incentives. If these factors have been included, they could manage the results of the outcomes negatively.

Stock trading is an additional idea to be continuous. For you to oversee that destiny agreement of trade, it means that the securities will preserve even on the next date. If the stocks have been not continuous, then it would pose a danger to the one's traders with buying shares at future expectations.

POWER PRINCIPLES TO ENSURE A STRONG ENTRY INTO DAY TRADING OPTIONS

Power Principle #1 – Ensure Good Money Management

Money is the tool that keeps the engine of the financial industry performing in good working order. It is essential that you learn to manage your money in a way that works for you instead of against you as an options day trader. It is an intricate part of managing your risk and increasing your profit.

Money management is the process whereby monies are allocated for spending, budgeting, saving, investing, and other processes. Money management is a term that any person with a career in the financial industry, and particularly in the options trading industry, is intimately familiar with because this allocation of funds is the difference between a winning options trader and a struggling options trader.

Below you will find tips for managing your money so that you have maximum control of your options day trading career.

Money Management Tips for Options Traders

- Define money goals for the short term and the long

term, so that you can envision what you would like to save, invest, etc. Ensure that these are recorded and easily accessed. Your trading plan will help you define your money goals.

- Develop an accounting system. There are wide ranges of software that can help with this, but it does not matter which one you use as long as you are able to establish records and easily track the flow of your money.

- Use the position sizing to manage your money. Position sizing is the process of determining how much money will be allocated to entering an options position. To do this effectively, allocated a smart percentage of your investment funds toward individual options. For example, it would be unwise to use 50% of your investment fund on one option. That is 50% of your capital that can potentially go down the drain if you make a loss in that position. A good percentage is using no more than 10% of your investment fund toward individual option positions. This percentage allocation will help you get through tough periods, which eventually happen without having all your funds being lost.

- NEVER, ever invest money that you cannot afford to lose. Do not let emotion override this principle and cloud your judgment.

- Spread your risks by diversifying your portfolio. You diversify your portfolio by spreading your wealth by investing in different areas; add to your investments regularly, being aware of commissions at all times, and knowing when to close a position.

- Develop the day trading styles and strategies that earn you a steady rate of return. Even if you use scalping where the returns are comparatively small, that steady flow of profit can add up big over time.

Power Principle #2 – Ensure That Risks and Rewards Are Balanced

To ensure that losses are kept to a minimum and that returns are as great as they can be, options day traders should use the risk/reward ratio to determine each and to make adjustments as necessary. The risk/reward ratio is an assessment used to show the profit potential with potential losses. This requires knowing the potential risks and profits associated with an options trade. Inherent risks are managed by using a stop-loss order. A stop-loss order is a command that allows you to exit a position in an options trade once a certain price threshold has been reached.

Profit is targeted using an established plan. The potential profit is calculated by finding the difference between the entry price and the target profit. This is calculated by dividing the expected return on the options investment by the standard deviation.

Another way to manage risks and rewards is by diversifying your portfolio. Always spread your money across different assets, financial sectors, and geographies. Ensure that these different facets of your portfolio are not closely related to each other so that if one goes down, they do not all fall. Be smart about protecting and building your wealth.

Power Principle #3 – Develop A Consistent Monthly Options Trading System

The aim of doing options trading daily is to have an overall winning options trading month. That will not happen if you trade options here and there. You cannot expect to see a huge profit at the end of the month if you only performed 2 or 3 transactions.

It would help if you had a high options trading frequency to up the chances of coming out winning every month. The only way to do that is to develop a system where you perform options trades at least five days a week.

To have consistently good months, you need to develop strong daily systems that keep your overall monthly average high. Therefore, creating a daily options trading schedule is vital. Here is an example of an efficient options day trading schedule:

1. **Perform market analysis.** This needs to be done before the markets open in the morning. That means that the options day trader needs to get an early start on the day. This entails checking the news to scan for any major events that might affect the markets that day, checking the economic calendar; and assessing the actions of other day traders to assess volume and competition.

2. **Manage your portfolio.** The way that an options day trader does this is dependent on the strategies that he or she implements, but overall, it is about assessing positions that you already have or are contemplating for efficient management of entry and exits that day. It also allows for good money management.

3. **Enter new positions.** After assessing the market and fine-tuning your portfolio, the next step is to enter new trades that day. Research and efficient decision-making go into this step. The options trader who has already determined how the market was doing and forecasted for performance that day would have noticed relevant patterns. The key here is to enter trades frequently via a sound strategy. To narrow done which positions you would like to pursue, keep an eye on the bullish, bearish, neutral and volatile watch lists, and run technical scans.

4. **Incorporate learning during the day.** Continual learning is something that an options trader needs to pursue, but this does not always have to be in the way of formal classes or courses. You can up your knowledge of options and day trading by following mentors, reading books, listening to podcasts, reading blogs, and watching videos online. Such activities are easy to incorporate into your daily routine. Even just a few minutes of study a day can go considerably up your options day trading game in addition to stimulating your mind. Being in regular contact with other options day traders is also a great way of

increasing your information well.

Power Principle #4 – Consider A Brokerage Firm That Is Right for Your Level of Options Expertise

I want to stress how important this decision is on an options day trader's profit margin. There are four important factors that you need to consider when choosing a broker and they are:

- The requirements for opening a cash and margin account.
- The unique services and features that the broker offers.
- The commission fees and other fees charged by the broker.
- The reputation and level of options expertise of the broker.

Let's take a look at these individual components to see how you can use them to power up your options day trading experience.

Broker Cash and Margin Accounts

Every options trader needs to open a cash account and margin account to be able to perform transactions. They are simply tools of the trade. A cash account is one that allows an options day trader to perform transactions via being loaded with cash. Margin accounts facilitate transactions by allowing that to borrow money against the value of security in his or her account. Both of these types of accounts require that a minimum amount be deposited. This can be as few as a few thousand dollars to tens of thousands of dollars, depending on the broker of choice. You need to be aware of the requirements when deliberating, which brokerage firm is right for you.

Broker Services and Features

There are different types of services and features available from various brokerage firms. For example, if an options trader would like to have an individual broker assigned to him or her to handle his or her account personally, then he or she will have to look for a full-service broker. In this instance, there minimum account requirements that need to be met. Also, commission fees and other fees are generally higher with these types of brokerage firms. While the fees are higher, this might be better for a beginner trader to have that full service dedicated to their needs and the learning curve.

On the other hand, if an options trader does not have the capital needed to meet the minimum requirements of a full-service broker or would prefer to be more in charge of his or her option trades, then there is the choice of going with a discount brokerage firm. The advantage to discount brokerage firms is that they tend to have lower commissions and fees. Most internet brokerage firms are discount brokers.

Other features that you need to consider when choosing a brokerage firm include:

- Whether or not the broker streams real-time quotes.
- The speed of execution for claims.

- The availability of bank wire services.
- The availability of monthly statements.
- How confirmations are done, whether written or electronic.

Commissions and Other Fees

Commission fees are paid when an options trader enters and exits positions. Every brokerage firm has its commission fees set up. These are typically developed around the level of account activity and account size of the options trader.

These are not the only fees that an option trader needs to consider when considering brokerage firms. Many brokerage firms charge penalty fees for withdrawing funds and not maintaining minimum account balances—obviously, the existence of fees such as these cuts on any options trader's profit margin. The payment of fees needs to be kept to a minimum to gain maximum income, and as such, an options trader needs to be aware of all fees that exist and how they are applied when operating with a brokerage firm. This needs to be done before signing up.

Power Principle #5 – Ensure That Exits Are Automated

Even though I have stated that emotions should be set aside when trading options, we are all human, and emotions are bound to come into the equation at some point. Knowing this, systems must be developed to minimize the impact of emotions. Having your exits automated is one such step that you can take to ensure that emotions are left out when dealing with options day trading. Using bracket orders facilitates this.

A bracket order is an instruction given when an options trader enters a new position that specifies a target or exit and stop-loss order that aligns with that. This order ensures that a system is set up to record two points – the target for-profit and the maximum loss point that will be tolerated before the stop-loss comes into effect. The execution of either order cancels the other.

MONEY MANAGEMENT

A s a trader, you have to develop specific skills, and one of these is money management. Learning how to trade is essential, but money management is equally important. Money management is all about keeping as much of your money as possible and not losing any of it unnecessarily.

As a trader, you do not have any control over the markets, but you can control your money and reduce your losses and any wastage. Money management is just as important as your trading skills. No matter how impressive and on-point your trading skills are, without money management skills, you will not thrive and will be a huge risk. Therefore, learn and understand all the essential aspects of money management.

The main purpose of money management is to ensure that each risk you take is a calculated risk and not guesswork. Every move that you make on the trading platform should be well researched, well informed, and guided by your analysis. Never make any guesswork or blind moves as you risk losing your money. It is better to hold out a little longer from entering a trade rather than lose money blindly.

As the experts say, the key to winning at the stock market losing as little money as possible If you are not right. Some of the critical considerations that you should make as a trader are the number of shares you should buy and the amounts to spend per trade.

Importance of Proper Money Management Skills

As a trader, one of the most essential skills you will need to develop is how to manage your money correctly and how to keep as much of it as possible. It would help if you learned how to save as much of your money as possible and avoid entering trades where you risk losing money. If you are unsure about a strategy, then do not implement it.

Your most crucial goal as a trader should be to preserve and protect your trading capital. This will enable you to last longer and grow your wealth and make big wins. For instance, there is a general rule that you should never spend more than 2% of your trading capital on a single trade. This means that if your trading capital is $100, 000 then no single trade should take more than $2,000. This way, should things not work in your favor, then you stand to lose as little as possible.

Also, no matter how enticing or attractive a position seems, never place a more significant amount than initially planned. Market positions on charts sometimes seem way too appealing, and we are inclined to invest more money for higher returns. However, the markets can be unpredictable, and chances of losing money or trades not working out as desired are always high. Therefore, avoid such temptations and stick to your trading plan.

Also, check your account balance each month and then work out the amount that makes 2% of the total. For instance, if your account balance is $50,000, then 2% is equivalent to $1,000. As a swing trader, you cannot afford to lose more than this amount. This kind of approach will enable you to hold onto most of your money as well as stay safe even as you trade. Keep in mind that the premise of the swing trading strategy is to collect profits on half of each position's amount as soon as the stock moves and gains an amount that is equivalent to the original stop loss.

Maintain Proper Cash Flow Management

Always have a very sound and well-thought-out cash flow process. This is probably one of the most crucial elements of long-term investment planning. It is a straightforward approach. All you need to do is to deposit money regularly into your accounts. This money can be used to buy more shares for long-term benefits.

Setting Target and Stops

We can define a stop-loss as the total amount of loss that a trader is willing to incur in a single trade. Beyond the stop-loss point, the trader exits the trade. This is meant to prevent further losses by thinking the trade will eventually get some momentum. We also have what is known as a take-profit point. It is at this point that you will collect any profits made and possibly exit a trade. At this point, stock or other security is often very close to the point of resistance. Beyond this point, a reversal in price is likely to take place. Rather than lose money, it would help if you exited the trade. Traders sometimes take profit and let trade continue if it was still making money. Another take-profit point is then plotted. If you have a good run, then you can lock in the profits and let the excellent run continue.

Always Have A Trading Plan

The single most crucial aspect of your trade should be risk management. Without it, your whole trading life will be in jeopardy. Therefore, start all your trading ventures with a plan that you intend to stick by. Traders have a saying that you should plan your trades and then trade your plan. This means to come up with the best plan possible and then implement it and stick by it. Trade is very similar to war. When it is well planned, it can be won before it is executed.

Some of the best tools you will need as part of your risk management plan are take-profit and stop-loss. Using these two tools, you can plan your trades. You will need to use technical analysis to determine these two points. With this information, you should be able to decide on the price you are willing to pay as well as the losses you can incur.

Risk Versus Reward

A lot of traders lose a lot of money at the markets for a straightforward reason. They do not know about risk management or how to go about it. This mostly happens to beginners or novice traders. Most of them learn how to trade, then rush to the markets in the hope of making a kill. Sadly, this is now how things work because account and risk management are not taken into consideration.

Managing risk is just as significant as learning how to trade profitably. It is a skill that every trader needs to discover, including beginners and novice traders. As it is, investing hard-earned funds at the markets can be a risky venture. Even with the very best techniques and latest software programs, you can still lose money. Experts also lose money at the markets occasionally. The crucial aspect is that they win a lot more than they lose, so the net equation is profitability.

Since trading is a risky affair, traders should be handsomely compensated for the risks they take. This is where the term risk vs. reward ratio comes in. If you are going to invest your money in a venture that carries some risk, then it is good to understand the nature of the risk. If it is too risky, then you may want to keep away, but if not, then perhaps the risk is worth it.

Financial Dashboards

A financial dashboard is a management tool commonly used by swing traders and other traders as well. It is mostly used for fast comparative analysis of major indicator data visually.

The data is often in the form of trend diagrams that are in series form, usually side-by-side. This tool is among the many useful tools that all traders should have if they need to compare market information fast.

A financial dashboard can accommodate huge amounts of data and organize it in such a way that it is easy to visualize it and make fast decisions based on the visualization. A wide variety of data can be formatted and presented to you as you prepared to trade and even as you trade. You will be able to proceed with more accuracy and make informed decisions.

Major Indicators for Stock Traders

As a stock trader, you will need to use a whole bunch of tools. Most of these tools will help to guide you in your stock trading ventures. Some of the best trading indicators or tools are those that will help in the identification of suitable stocks for trading. They include tools that will enable you to identify best market entry points, management of your market positions, and also for-profit collection and market exit.

Fibonacci Retracement

One of the best tools used by most traders, including swing traders, is the Fibonacci retracement pattern. This pattern is used mostly to identify resistance and support levels. When these support and resistance levels are known, it is possible to determine the reversals and hence, appropriate market entry points.

Stocks generally retrace their path a short while after trending either upwards or downwards. The market entry point is often deemed best as soon as the retracement is over, and the trend is resumed. The retracements are generally measured as percentages. Swing traders usually watch out for the 50% market, which is rather significant even though it does not exactly fit in with the Fibonacci pattern. Fibonacci is often at ratios ranging from 23.6% and 38.2% all the way to 61.8%.

Pullbacks

By their very nature, pullbacks always generate a variety of different trading opportunities after a trend moves lower or higher. Profiting through this classic strategy is not as easy as it sounds. For instance, you may invest in a security or sell short into a resistance position, and these trends can continue so that your losses are considerable. Alternatively, your safety or stock could just sit there and waste away, even as you miss out on many other opportunities.

There are specific skills you need if you are to earn decent profits with the pullback strategy. For instance, how aggressive should a trader be, and at what point should profit be taken? When is it time to pull out? These and all other important aspects should be considered.

For starters, you require a strong trend on the markets such that other traders' timing pullbacks get to line up right behind you. When they do, they will cause your idea to become a profitable one. Securities that ascend to new heights or falling to new lows are capable of attaining this requirement, especially after the securities push much farther beyond the breakout level.

You will also need persistent vertical action into a trough or peak for regular profits, especially if the volumes are higher than usual, mainly because this results in a fast price movement once you attain the position. The stock in question must turn a profit quickly after either bottoming or topping out but with no sizable trade range or consolidation. It is also crucial that this happens. Otherwise, the intervening range is likely to oppose profitability during the resulting subsequent rollover or bounce.

Resistance and Support Triggers

There are lines known as support and resistance points that form the core of the technical analysis. It is easy to build a trading plan using these indicators. The first one is the support line, and it is a good indicator of the price level. It also indicates areas below prevailing market prices on the chart with strong buying pressure.

CPSIA information can be obtained
at www.ICGtesting.com
Printed in the USA
BVHW060940151121
621686BV00002B/102